inner thoughts of a habromaniac

raven unilowski

BookLeaf Publishing

Presentation by *BookLeaf Publishing*

Web: www.bookleafpub.com

E-mail: info@bookleafpub.com

ISBN: 9789357211598

First edition 2023

DEDICATION

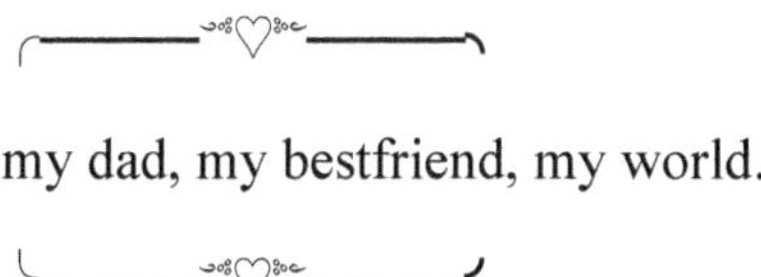

my dad, my bestfriend, my world.

ACKNOWLEDGEMENT

you thought of me as your world,
i see you as mine, now more than ever.
not a day goes by without thinking of you.
i cannot fathom nor grasp
your designated departure,
your absence from this earth.
i miss you.

i cannot thank you enough.
you taught me how to love, how to laugh,
how to be strong, to not be fearful, to take things
lightly, to care, to live and be in the moment.

i will bury your existence with me.
i will forever mourn.
i love you.

♡

PREFACE

you're dying wish was for me
to live happily.
i'm not quite sure if that has
added up to your expectations
or even mine yet.
some days i think i am happy.
i want to experience it, truly.
however sadness is comforting.
it feels like home.
it has been the home inside my head
for as long as i can remember.
ever since i was a little girl.
the smile on my face often captures
in glimpses off camera.
these are compilations of the
thoughts that bury itself in my head,
that swim and ponder in circles until
they escape and seap onto paper
brewing in pen ink.
these are the drafts of a habromaniac.

to whoever's flame this may ignite,
    i hope it keeps you warm.
      you are not alone ♡

happy birthday dad

today you would have been 67.
to me you are 67 and no longer 63.
you were born on a tuesday, as was i.
i know by 8:00am on the dot
we would be having strawberry milkshakes
at a booth, in a denny's.
you would be reading the paper,
while i watch instant replays
of football on the tv.
until it's my turn to skim through
the comics and astrology readings.
we'd make comment on one that
features garfield or charlie brown.
on our way out you'd be making
conversation with the host
leaving them a joke,
paired with a smile
on both of your faces.
your presence filled every room
with light that would eventually linger
when you would depart.
you were never dull in my eyes.
on the drive over to best buy
you would turn on the radio
requesting i choose the station
to set the vibe for the day.

you were always happy regardless
of what was picked.
i loved your open mindedness
towards music
and the variety you've fulfilled
your ears with over time.
how i will never get to thank you
enough for showing me such diversity
and true passion of what makes
music so riveting to the heart.
for that was one of the strongest things
that could make our bond

   so connected

all we had to do was
turn the volume to full
and nod our heads with a grin.
no words required.
we could read each other
in complete silence.
which never stopped to amaze me.

— raven unilowski

these are the few tricks up your sleeve

go ahead
run away
my words and thoughts
won't make you stay.
you're not walking on a tight rope
nor chained to a leash.
i just wanted things to end in peace.
each day i wake up
i fall to my knees
you brush me off like it's a breeze.

fall is over
for i am just dead abandoned leaves.
the nights i manage to get sleep,
i have dreams.
it's barely enough for me to grieve.
if only you weren't such a tease,
it would relieve me to feel once at ease.
did you know i have needs too?
crease my fragile heart
and crush the seeds that could have grew.

please,
as if it's not winter now,
you willingly let me freeze.
oh how i wish that were an
option for my thoughts.
you lost the keys to my loving lock.

in hopes that you leave

    never forgotten,

        these are the few tricks up your sleeve.

— raven unilowski

bad habits

my visions in red,
my hearts in blue.
days like this are where
i can't catch a clue.
you're a mess,
that's something i do.
the way i attach myself,
it's just like glue.

— raven unilowski

reunited visions

63.9 trips around the sun
    and 16.5 spent with you ♡

one day i will be able to reunite with you
to officially share another sunrise, another
milkshake, another comic reading, another
x-men marathon and movie day all over.

until then.

— raven unilowski

another shower thought discovery

i've discovered why i don't always feel myself
and it's because i am changing.
so how can i ever be myself?
when i don't stay the same.
i never fail to mention to people that
change is necessary to being whole.
i have failed to put that piece to my
own very puzzle until now.
i had a love hate relationship with change
i'm sure many people do.
you do need to step out of your
comfort zone for these
things to become reality.
i was at a point where change did not
fulfill me or comfort.
it scared me to cross a line,
 a boundary,
i had not set for myself.
i will never be fully whole nor complete
due to the constance of my change
and of my being.
i have learned to accept that.
i will create many different versions of myself
and i will love them all as they come and go,

until they last.
change is necessary,
change is you.
changes in you are whole
and what is whole is yourself.
be yourself.

——— raven unilowski

sunset

i watched the sun go down.
not in contact eye to eye.
just sitting in my bedroom
staring at the walls
and ceiling.
from the warmest fulfilment of light
peer through my window
to merely reflections
upon silhouettes
of the ruinous nocturnal affliction.
it all went by so fast.
my mind is no longer steady,
how could i have let myself
sit this long
without?

— raven unilowski

time thinner

to fill the line
that's left behind,
because it's only a matter of time.

— raven unilowski

wounds of adrenaline

i tore a slivered piece of skin off my finger.

didn't even flinch.
i watched the blood rush out of the gap between
layers
i had just exposed to thin air.
my hand is numb
my brain is in shock.
the shaking in my fingers won't stop,
pure adrenaline of the nerves.
is this the pain i crave for or i lack,
is this what i deserve?
maybe all of the above.
is this my daily test of reality?
who i am, i say i am?
what i look straight into the
mirror at everyday?
warmth increases,
bloods pumping faster.
wish i could experience that intensity
for a head rush.
this is adrenaline in the finger tips.

— raven unilowski

rulings of a flame

ignite your strengths,
burn your weaknesses.
your passion and love
are forever eternal.

— raven unilowski

oblivion

live from fear,
of the possible outcomes
of the unknown.

— raven unilowski

mental games

try to stay afloat,
the heavy weight of disaster
is upon your awakening each day.
it's your continuous destined battle.
for you are the chosen one.
your awareness is your shield
and your reaction is your weapon.
make it how you wish,
how you desire.
to perceive your being of reflection
face to face with glass.
transparency.
how your heart is so cold and distant
like it's no longer.
it's hollow.
how do you cope with sorrow?
do you ever have enough in you to weap?
shed one last tear?
do your thoughts linger?
follow along with your finger.
tracing with a blade
mark your territory of pain.
of depth,
close to the bone.
your nerves tingle

you really think this is
what you deserve?

— raven unilowski

to live and forget

let us slip away to a journey that's not ours.
scattered stars among the lines
of connect the dots.
merge our hearts under the darkened sky
we both view from below,
colliding our thoughts and our lips as we
forsaken this night good bye.

— raven unilowski

mournings after

life gets kind of crazy
been declining calls lately,
no it ain't that easy.
i find it hard to explain
you won't understand my pain.
yeah, it's okay.
maybe someday,
you'll just fade away.
i might see you in my dreams
knowing it's not reality.
tears on my pillowcase
mascara running down my face.

      put a smile on that face
         at least,
            that's what people say.

— raven unilowski

earth's breathtaker

the perfect picture doesn't exist.
staring at your watch,
memory fades
the time in bliss.
you're constantly
taking a piss
on life.
bittersweet, litter, tweet.
high on life.
human but i have nine lives,
derealization.
this isn't cloud nine.
complain, bitch, whine.
i think you need to rewind.
smoke the highest terpene.
snake, slither, serpentine.
peace is where the pine is
analyze your own biz.
i won't take no hits
that don't involve the mary jane,
i gain to feel no pain.
shits temporary.
the cold
like my love for januarys.

— raven unilowski

overflowing fountain

there's times where i don't care
if my phone dies.
i could care less.
i have a camera, notebook, music.
what more do i need?
i'm okay on my own.
with people i still feel just as empty.
my thoughts never escape my head.
it's just always replaced with
something new.
i question everything,
at times more than i should.
i can't help but to be so self aware
and never let my guard down.
too many people have proven to break
that barrier and completely ruin
the things between us.
sick and tired.
burnt out and fired.
why is the thought of you
engulfed in my head?
i want to go to bed.
i want to breathe.
breathe and feel at ease.
my mind wanders,

it simply can't do just that.
i want to be left alone.
i'm my only option.
there's nowhere left to go.
i have nothing, nowhere, nobody
to call my home.
people leave, they never stay.
don't make yourself at home
when i happen to linger
around your presence.
it's all temporary,
i am temporary.

— raven unilowski

lost in the snow

oh how i miss my home
how i miss my soul
how i feel so alone
now i feel so old
now i feel so cold.
seasons change
there's snow.
days go by
i'm on my own.

— raven unilowski

extensive solitude

this assumed authority over another?
self reminder.
you no longer fathom or dwell
on their well being.
days spent alone
are the days
your soul becomes
the most grown.
your heart once broken
becomes
stitched and sewed.

sorrow over bliss.
overcome this severed attachment
to the mind
break the cycle
this bottomless swimming pool.
it's clear to everyone else
but to you.
it's foggy, cold, shallow
deeply blindsided.
commonly bonded
with a start and finish line.
liars, bullshitters, too facers
they are not beyond those obstacles.

however,
everyone else broken
must be replaced from current reach.
out of context from the heartless.

— raven unilowski

i'm passing by time

i plead and beg myself
when will it end?
my days off are spent
overslept in bed.
the walls start to become
my new bestfriend.
i lose myself
in hell of endeavour.
losing grasp at hope.
windows cracked open
i smoke my dope.
seeking help is no longer an option
when you're trapped in your head,
it's a weary concoction.

— raven unilowski

sunset II

it's getting darker in my room
i don't know what to do,

but accept the darkness,
that the light no longer fades in.

— raven unilowski

object in the mirror

my thoughts drift and linger
numb from the tip of my finger.
i'm such an overthinker.
the negativity just gets bigger.
i can't escape,
my brains locked in a crate.
not crystal clear, it's opaque.
this is my mental state.
the liquor, i've been her.
picked her, it was bitter.
you get the gist.
just check my wrist.
do i even still exist?
what did i miss?
in the midst of it all
the amount of times
i stumble and fall.
did i end up risking it all?
am i facing a wooden wall
or this just a one way hall?
i don't get no phone calls
i've been forced to crawl.
yeah it's been a real long haul.

i am here.
not in the present, not in the future,

and nor in the past. i am here.
i am not in the moment, i am here.
life is a token, if i speak is it broken?
lessons are often taught unspoken.
it's got to be someone's slogan.
was i woken? my hearts frozen.
everything rolls in slow motion.
my devotion has been stolen.
my emotions cause commotion,
that's why my thoughts swim in the ocean.
it marinates in potion, the effects are corrosion. i
just want to be chosen.
it's all i ever wanted. to feel close and well
bonded. no one's ever responded.
this idea was subconsciously prompted.
to society it's just been discarded.

please just disregard it, maybe it's all in my
head. i overthink before bed. i recall what you
said, those are the texts that i've read.
i'm hanging on by a thread. i can't see what's
ahead. i can't swim so i fled. instead.
this isn't what i meant.
my words get twisted, they're bent
i wish i was content
i got nowhere to vent
i rarely feel, repent
all the time that i've spent.
it could have helped me prevent

not let it get to this extent.
the path is descent
i achieve to reinvent.
it's only a percent
it's under ferment
at least from what i last remember
it was right before fall, last september.
i used to lose my temper
now i cry and tremor.
semper for the worse
i can't put it all in one verse
my life feels like a curse
wish i could put it in reverse
time can't be reimbursed
so i let myself immerse and wither.

my soul belongs to the river
no home that can deliver
all snakes slither
it makes me shiver
so i reconsider
and put together the triggers
find the base transmitter
will it make me heal quicker
the leftover poison in pitcher
made by the love of sinners
so i sit here and quiver
i picked her.
i'm back where i belong

you were right
i'm wrong
are you gonna let this prolong
because i'm sick and done
of all the damage you run
you never let me see the sun
you won
you : one
me : none
i have nothing left.

my heart was wanted for theft
it no longer beats out of my chest
i'm alone and depressed
more like a guest and possessed
what more did i expect?
i got nothing to protect
it's been absorbed by neglect
i can't be more direct
i'm an object
a reject
subject to resurrect
according to you that's incorrect
i need to leave
i never get to grieve
the toxicity i receive
is what you led me to believe.

— raven unilowski

diminishing

not everyone will see this
it will linger in their minds
for a matter of seconds then
diminish
like no recollection of it
tomorrow,
the next day, the day after that,
or even the day after that.
not even july 16th 2027 or 2034.
tomorrow is not permanency.
it could exist for a split second
not everyone could experience it.
you or i could pass
swoon in the lively soil six feet under
embedded by an entrapment of wood
and cloth eternally bound to diminish.
i will disappear.
especially all of human society at
one point or another.
i do not care for the lack in my expression
of vocabulary.
i cannot remove these inevitable facts
brewing, seeping over my thoughts.
day and night, am and pm consistently.

my existence will go unnoticed, unrecognizable,
undeniably, purely.
nothing more than a speck of dust
on this elderly rich planet,
once i take my final and last breath.

— raven unilowski